Going Through a

FAMILY BREAKUP

Stories from Survivors

SARAH EASON AND SARAH LEVETE

CHERITON
CHILDREN'S BOOKS

Please visit our website, www.cheritonchildrensbooks.com to see more of our high-quality books.

First Edition

Published in 2022 by Cheriton Children's Books
PO Box 7258, Bridgnorth, Shropshire, WV16 9ET, UK

Authors: Sarah Eason and Sarah Levete
Designer: Paul Myerscough
Illustrator: Sylwia Filipczak
Editor: Jennifer Sanderson
Picture Researcher: Rachel Blount
Proofreader: Tracey Kelly

Picture credits: Cover: Sylwia Filipczak; Inside: p1: Shutterstock/Kamira; p4: Shutterstock/Fizkes; p5: Shutterstock/Khuncho24; p6: Shutterstock/Oleggg; p7: Shutterstock/Rido; p9: Shutterstock/Fizkes; p10: Shutterstock/Roman Kosolapov; p11: Shutterstock/Yulia Grigoryeva; p12: Shutterstock/Wavebreakmedia; p14: Shutterstock/Yakobchuk Viacheslav; p15: Shutterstock/UfaBizPhoto; p16: Shutterstock/LightField Studios; p18: Shutterstock/Fizkes; p19: Shutterstock/ Fizkes; p20: Shutterstock/Monkey Business Images; p22: Shutterstock/Prostock-studio; p24: Shutterstock/Kamira; p25: Shutterstock/Rawpixel.com; p26: Shutterstock/Zephyr_p; p27: Shutterstock/Fizkes; p29: Shutterstock/Sirtravelalot; p31: Shutterstock/Myboys.me; p32: Shutterstock/Red Umbrella and Donkey; p34: Shutterstock/Fizkes; p35: Shutterstock/Zivica Kerkez; p36: Shutterstock/ Fizkes; p38: Shutterstock/Dzmitry Malyeuski; p40: Shutterstock/Monkey Business Images; p41: Shutterstock/Jacob Lund; p42: Shutterstock/Tijana Moraca; p43: Shutterstock/Pixelheadphoto digitalskillet; p45: Shutterstock/Who is Danny.

Printed in the United States of America

Publisher's Note: The stories in this book are fictional stories based on extensive research of real-life experiences.

CONTENTS

CHAPTER ONE

WHEN A FAMILY BREAKS DOWN

Families are changing. Today, it is more common than ever before for families to break up. Attitudes to families are changing, too. These days, people are willing to accept new families that form from breakups much more easily than they did in the past. These families may be single parents sharing the care of their children or **blended families** and **foster families**. One thing that hasn't changed over the years, though, is how difficult it is to be a child caught up in a family breakup. The complex feelings and issues that young people experience in this situation can be very difficult to cope with.

WHY DO FAMILIES BREAK UP?

There are many reasons why families break up. Sometimes, couples fall out of love and no longer want to be together. Other times, situations can force a family breakup. These can include job or money problems and sometimes even **bereavement**. There is no single or simple way to understand and manage a family breakup, or one way to cope with it. Everyone will have different experiences and different reactions if their family has problems.

Families break down for many different reasons. Whatever the reason, the breakup is difficult for everyone involved.

Many young people struggle to cope when their family breaks up. Some struggle with difficult emotions, including sadness.

It Happened to Me

This book follows the "It Happened to Me" fictional journals of different young people going through a family breakup. These stories from survivors explain what it feels like when your family falls apart and how breakups happen. The conclusions to their stories on pages 44-45 also show that it is possible to get through a breakup and lead a happy and fulfilling life. The stories and information in this book can support people going through family problems and help everyone better understand what it is like to be in this situation.

HOW PEOPLE BREAK UP

There is no right or easy way for a family to break up. How it is done all depends on each individual in the family and the family's particular situation. All families are unique, and the way they break up will differ from one family to another. Despite what some people say, breaking up a family is never simple, painless, or easy for anyone. It is usually a difficult and painful process for everyone involved.

Family breakups can come about for many reasons. For example, some adult relationships sometimes end suddenly, and the couple may decide to split up immediately. Other times, the couple may decide to split up and then take their time setting up any practical arrangements. These may include where family members live and how their finances will be organized. It can also sometimes be the case that adults argue for a very long time before a breakup. They may be unhappy in their relationship for many years before they make the decision to stop living together and finally separate. This period of negativity within a family can be very distressing for children. They are often painfully aware of arguments, shouting, or lengthy silences. They may worry about their parents' relationship but feel unable to change it, despite seeing it unravel before their eyes. For any child in this situation, it is deeply unsettling.

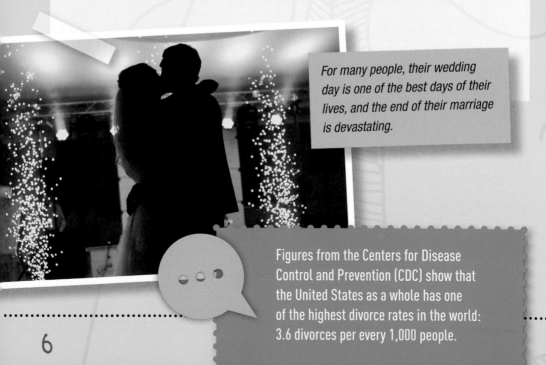

For many people, their wedding day is one of the best days of their lives, and the end of their marriage is devastating.

Figures from the Centers for Disease Control and Prevention (CDC) show that the United States as a whole has one of the highest divorce rates in the world: 3.6 divorces per every 1,000 people.

ENDING A MARRIAGE

Marriage is a legally binding relationship. This means that the relationship is recognized and protected by law. As a result, when a married couple decide to end their relationship and split up for good, they must go through a legal process to formally signal the end of their marriage. This is called a divorce. Cohabiting couples are people who live together but have never married. Unlike married couples, they can separate without finalizing the end of their relationship in law.

Everyone in a family benefits if the relationship between the parents is good.

IT HAPPENS

There is a lot of discussion in the media and society about the harmful effects of family breakups. Some people believe that parents should stay together "for the sake of the children," even if the couple are very unhappy. They believe that it is better for children to have two parents, no matter what the situation. Others argue that it is more damaging for children to live with adults who have a very troubled relationship. They believe that parents deserve happy, loving relationships. They also think that it is better for children to witness these types of relationships rather than unhealthy ones.

Nothing Will Ever Be OK Again

MONDAY SEPTEMBER 12

I can hear Mom yelling again. It's like this every day now. She screams at Dad that she is sick of having to be the one to pick up the pieces all the time, and that Dad takes no responsibility. I get what she is saying—ever since he lost his job, Dad has just been at home, doing nothing all day, while Mom goes to work. I don't think it's his fault, though, or that he is lazy. I think he is just really sad ...

THURSDAY OCTOBER 13

I heard Dad crying today while I was doing my homework, before Mom got home. I asked him what is wrong, but he just told me not to worry and that he is fine. But I can see he isn't. It just makes me worry more when he says that. When Mom came home, I told her that Dad is sad. She told me not to worry, too! What is wrong with them?! I just want to know what is going on. I talked to Cassie later. She said Mom and Dad are going to split up.

SATURDAY NOVEMBER 5

It's true. Mom and Dad are splitting up! Mom came into my bedroom just now and told me they are breaking up. She says it's not my fault—or Cassie's. It's just that she and Dad aren't getting along anymore, and that things have gotten worse and worse since Dad lost his job. I told Mom that Dad is sad and just needs to get better.

I said when Dad gets a job again, everything will be OK. But Mom wouldn't listen—she says splitting up is for the best. But it won't be best for me. I can't stop crying—why is Mom doing this to me, to all of us? I hate her.

Dad went to stay with Grandma and Grandpa. He gave me a big hug and cried as he left—I didn't want to let go of him. He says he will take me out next week and that we'll spend lots of time together. He says it will all be OK. But it's not going to be OK—nothing will ever be OK again.

I wish it would stop —all my parents do is scream and fight.

CHAPTER TWO

BREAKING DOWN

There are countless reasons why a relationship breaks down and parents decide to part. For example, sometimes, problems in a relationship may develop over a long period of time and finally cause a split. Other times, the problem is unexpected, and the breakup is sudden and seemingly out of the blue.

WANTING TO KNOW WHY

Children often want to know the exact reason why parents separate. They may hope that if a specific problem can be found for the relationship breakdown, it can be fixed and the breakup stopped. However, in many cases, there may not be one specific cause. Instead, there may be many different problems that build up over time. Sadly, it may be impossible to **resolve** them, despite the best intentions of the parents.

Couples who marry young are much more likely to break up than older couples.

Sometimes, there is no obvious explanation for a breakup. This can be particularly difficult for children to come to terms with. After all, it is bad enough to have to watch your family falling apart if you know the reason why, but when no one can tell you why that is happening it is even harder to hard to bear. What causes family breakups will also differ from one family to the next. It all depends on each unique situation.

DEALING WITH A BREAKUP

There is no right or wrong time for parents to part. For example, young children may be less aware of what is happening when their parents split up. However, when they are older, it can take some time to come to terms with their experience. Some children may have spent most of their time with one parent only before a breakup. In these cases, they may not experience the direct sense of loss that many children feel when one parent leaves. However, they may still need to deal with their difficult feelings.

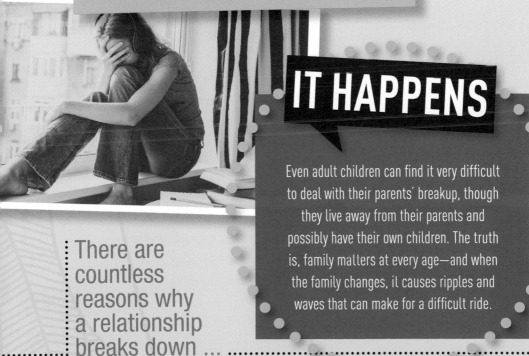

Children can feel that the breakup is all their fault. It is important that parents explain to their children that they are not to blame.

IT HAPPENS

Even adult children can find it very difficult to deal with their parents' breakup, though they live away from their parents and possibly have their own children. The truth is, family matters at every age—and when the family changes, it causes ripples and waves that can make for a difficult ride.

There are countless reasons why a relationship breaks down ...

ARGUMENTS AND BREAKUPS

All couples argue from time to time. This is completely normal, and every partnership has its ups and downs. Thankfully, parents are usually able to resolve these problems, and their relationship gets past them. However, in some instances, the arguments only seem to get worse. The parents grow angrier and more and more distant from each other. Sadly, this can kind of ongoing conflict can lead to a breakup.

UPS AND DOWNS

People fall in love—and sometimes they fall out of love, for no particular reason. For example, one parent may meet someone else by chance and fall in love. Over time, they may decide that they want to leave their current relationship and live with the person that they are now in love with. However, it is important for children to always remember that when a parent stops loving their partner, it doesn't mean they no longer love their child or children. That love is **unconditional** and does not change, no matter what happens to the parents' relationship.

Couples who argue all the time may decide to separate, so that their children will not experience constant conflict.

Figures from the US Bureau of the Census show a high rate of breakup in second and third marriages. Forty-one percent of first marriages end in divorce, 60 percent of second marriages end in divorce, and 73 percent of third marriages end in divorce.

PEOPLE UNDER PRESSURE

Stress and worry can make a person moody and difficult to live with. For example, they may become **withdrawn** or lack interest in others, or they may become argumentative and easily pick fights with other family members. A person who suffers from **depression** or another mental health issue often finds it difficult to be involved and engaged with family activity. They can seem distant and unloving, but this does not mean that they do not care about the people in their family. They are simply struggling to cope with everyday life. However, this behavior can put a huge strain on the other parent, who often then takes on the responsibility of dealing with the family alone, with little support from their partner. In other situations, one parent may find a partner's drug or alcohol abuse too harmful and difficult to deal with and, as a result, reluctantly decide to end the relationship and separate.

Many parents also argue about money—what should be spent on what or whom, and how much! They may have different views about what things should be given priority. These disagreements can expose even deeper cracks in the relationship, cracks that the parents may feel unable to repair.

IT HAPPENS

Money worries can put an enormous strain on relationships. However, despite this, reports show that the divorce rate actually falls when a country's economy dips and rises when its economy improves. Could this unexpected occurrence be because of the financial consequences of running two households in the case of a divorce and the heavy cost of hiring lawyers to end a marriage?

"Mom and Dad said they still love me, and nothing will change that."

HARMING CHILDREN

The terrible and ugly truth is that some adults are **abusive** toward their partner or child. This abuse can take many forms. It may be physical violence, sexual abuse, or **psychological** bullying. None of these forms of abuse is acceptable in any circumstances. In cases of abuse, a child should try to find a trusted adult with whom they feel safe and tell them what is happening at home. The child can then be given the support and attention they need to be safe from harm and begin to get over the abuse and its damaging effects.

THE PRICE CHILDREN PAY

Children often find it difficult to talk to trusted adults about what is happening to them when they are victims of abuse at home. They may worry that telling someone about abuse will lead to the breakup of their family. As a result, they remain silent about the harm that is being done to them. However, it is much more important for children to find the support and safety they need and deserve than to risk their physical or emotional well-being in an attempt to hold their family together. A child's safety and happiness should always come first.

Witnessing their parents fighting can be terrifying and traumatic for children.

SUFFERING IN MANY WAYS

Children who are exposed to
family violence may well suffer
from depression as a result of
the abuse. Later, they may also
become victims or **abusers**
in their adult relationships.
Of course, it is important to
remember that many children are incredibly
resilient and are not affected in this way at all.
However, sadly, some children are, and people
argue that if they were not exposed to the abuse
when young they may well not have become
abusers themselves in adulthood. Children often feel
intense anxiety and fear when they witness one dearly loved parent
being abused. They may also feel guilty for not interfering and trying
to stop the abuse. No child should have to experience this situation.

A study by the Department
of Justice showed that
one-quarter of children in
the United States witnessed
some sort of domestic
violence in one year.

IT HAPPENS

People sometimes wonder why an abused parent
doesn't simply leave a violent household. In reality,
it is often very hard for the victim to leave. She (and
less often he) may fear that her safety and that of her
children will be threatened even more if she leaves.
The abusive partner may control the household's
finances, leaving the abused partner with no money
or shelter if she attempts to leave. Thankfully, there
are now organizations that work to protect the well-
being of people fleeing **domestic abuse**.

A CHILD'S VIEWPOINT

One of the first things that young people often wonder when they discover that their parents are separating is "Who will live with whom?" Parents often make the decision about living arrangements without consulting their children. The children may feel this **resolution** is very unfair, believing that they should have a say in what happens to them. After all, it is their lives that are changing because of the decisions that their parents have made, not them! However, should a child be given the right to decide with whom they live? Is this practical when considering the enormous implications involved in family breakups, such possible **relocation**? These are difficult questions and ones for which, unfortunately, there is no easy answer.

Ideally, parents will always take a child's views into account when making a decision about whom they live with and where. However, it may not always be possible or even in the best interests of the child to act on those views. Each situation is different, and parents will try to come to the best arrangement possible for their children, even though their children may find the outcome upsetting initially.

It's not always easy, but it's important that both moms and dads try to keep up strong relationships with their children after a breakup.

"I didn't want to choose—
I love Mom and Dad the same."

According to figures from America's Families and Living Arrangements, 69.4 percent of American children live with both parents, 23.1 percent live with their mother only, 3.4 percent live with their father only, and 4.1 percent live with neither parent.

Some campaign groups in the United States, such as Fathers4Justice®, protest against **judgments** by family courts. The fathers in the campaign groups believe that too many decisions are made in favor of mothers and that the fathers' importance in their children's lives is not sufficiently recognized. These campaign groups use stunts such as dressing up in superhero outfits and hanging from cranes to raise awareness for their cause.

MOTHER OR FATHER?

Usually, during a family breakup, children are more likely to stay with their mother than their father. However, many children do live with their fathers. Sometimes, parents agree on joint parenting. In this case, the children live with one parent and regularly stay with the other. This arrangement is called shared parenting, and it means that children spend time with both parents. However, it is not always the easiest option—it means two bedrooms, two toothbrushes, and often two sets of rules as children split their time between two homes.

Sometimes **custody** is awarded to one parent alone, with the other parent having little or no **access** to the child or children. In these instances, the parent may not be in a position to care for their children. This inability to care for the children can be for a variety of reasons. For example, the parent may have an alcohol or drug problem that needs to be dealt with before they can safely care for a child once more.

CAUGHT IN THE MIDDLE

Divorcing or separating parents can usually come to an agreement about the care of their children, who are, after all, the most precious part of their family. However, in some instances, this resolution is not possible. A great deal of external help may be required to find a solution and arrive at an arrangement that all parties can accept.

Having to share their time between two parents can be very traumatic for children.

Sometimes, parents may go to the courts to ask for help in making decisions about child custody arrangements or access to their children. In these cases, the needs of the child should be at the forefront of any decisions about contact with parents, no matter how convincing a parent may be in their argument about retaining custody. In some cases, a court will grant a parent only limited contact with their child. This decision may be related to safety and child well-being issues or other important concerns. However, even though they may have been made for reasonable and well-intentioned reasons, it is not always easy for family members to accept and live with such decisions.

IT HAPPENS

Some children may live with only one parent or with relatives for reasons unrelated to the breakdown of their parents' relationship. There can be many reasons why families change, such as the death of a parent. In these situations, some of the feelings surrounding family breakup may be relevant. However, there may also be different issues for those family members to come to terms with.

STEPPING IN TO HELP

Mediation is an important and valuable part of the process of deciding custody cases. It can often be used to help people avoid the personal trauma and financial cost of going to court. In mediation cases, a professional acts as a "middle person" between the parents. The mediator tries to help them put aside arguments and anger, so that they can calmly and sensibly talk about how to resolve their issues and find solutions to their problems. Instead of shouting, the parents are encouraged to come to an agreement that is in the best interests of their children.

TORN IN TWO

When parents argue over access or custody, children often feel torn between the two people whom they love the most. Parents may say unkind things about each other to their children or try and influence their views. This behavior is unfair: The relationship breakdown is between the adults, not the children. Children should be able to love both parents without fear of upsetting one or the other.

Sometimes, couples need a person outside of the family to help them resolve their issues.

DEALING WITH CHANGE

Change seems to affect everything when a family breaks up. There is huge emotional upheaval and confusion, but there are also a lot of practical changes to make and adjust to. It often seems to young people that the changes affect them the most, without them even wanting the changes. They may feel that they are not given any choice about what happens to them, or that they are involved in the decision-making process that brought about the changes.

The implications of family breakups are significant. For example, both parents may need to leave the family home and live in new places as a result of financial or practical problems, or a combination of both. This relocation may mean moving away from an area where the family was comfortable and happy to a different location where everything is new and both parents and children have to start over. If a parent moves a considerable distance, then young people may have to change schools, even if they are partway through a year of study. The relocation can be an extremely hard blow. It forces the children involved to leave their friends and begin the process of making new ones, just at a time when they feel most in need of their trusted friendships.

Continuing to do regular things such as playing sports can help children when everything else in their lives is changing.

IT HAPPENS

When a family breakup takes place, it is important to remember that it is the situation that changes, not the people. Friends, family, and brothers and sisters remain the same. Physical distance doesn't break friendships or relationships. It does require flexibility, however, and means finding new ways to keep in touch. Thankfully, today's technology means that it is easier than ever to maintain regular contact with friends who can offer the support young people need at this challenging time.

BROTHERS AND SISTERS

Every child in the family will feel differently about their parents' separation. For example, one child may feel angry if a brother or sister seems to be siding with one parent. They may also feel torn between their parents and under pressure to take sides, too, despite not wanting to. It's natural to have conflicting reactions in this difficult situation. However, it's important to respect each other's viewpoint.

TOUGH FOR PARENTS, TOO

The impact of separation and divorce is hard on parents as well as their children. What was once a shared daily responsibility of caring for a family becomes the responsibility of just one parent when the children are living with them. This can be very hard, and the parent left with the daily care of a child or children may not always get it right. It can take time to adjust to the situation and take on board everyone's needs and viewpoints.

I Hate Mom for Doing This

MONDAY SEPTEMBER 13

It's been a month now since Mom left. Dad has hardly stopped crying. He keeps telling me that he is OK, but he isn't! I wish he'd be honest with me. I've been trying to help out more, looking after Jake and playing with him. He keeps asking where Momma is. I've told him she has gone on vacation, and she'll be back soon. Total lie, but Jake sucks it up. Mom's been depressed since she had Jake—and now she's gone. I hate Mom for doing this.

THURSDAY OCTOBER 7

Mom's sister, my Aunt Julie, has moved in to help us for a little while. Mom is staying with a friend for now. Mom called me today. She cried on the phone and told me that she loves me, loves Jake, too. She says she just can't deal with being at home right now, and she needs a break from everything. I felt numb when she talked to me. It's like nothing touches me now.

I feel so angry at Mom—I can't stand it anymore.

Aunt Julie gave me a big hug after. She says it's normal to have different feelings, and that there is nothing wrong with me—I'm just going through a lot. Dad and Aunt Julie were talking later—Dad kept holding his head in his hands and saying that it isn't going to work with Mom.

SATURDAY DECEMBER 4

I saw Mom today. She gave me a huge hug and cried and cried. She scooped up Jake and kissed him all over his face. He laughed and kissed her back. Lucky Jake. He doesn't hate Mom like I do. We walked in the park, and Mom told me she is feeling a lot better. Her doctor is helping her with medication, and she is doing better every day. She says she even has a job now. I said, "Good for you, Mom. Your new life sounds great! Shame you've forgotten your family!" Aunt Julie told me not to be cruel. Mom cried. I don't care. I hate her.

SUNDAY JANUARY 2

Aunt Julie has been talking to Dad and Mom, trying to help them patch things up. Dad said he didn't want to see Mom, to go through all that with her again. But Aunt Julie said Mom was so much better now, and things would be different this time. Dad met Mom a few times to talk, and he came home really happy. He says Mom isn't sick anymore, and she is like she used to be before she had Jake. Yeah, right ...

Mom moved back in today. Dad keeps grinning like an idiot. So does Jake. He keeps giggling and cuddling Mom. They are both losers. Don't they get it? She'll only do it again. Who leaves their kids like that? I don't believe she ever really loved us ...

CHAPTER THREE

DEALING WITH FEELINGS

Parents going through a separation or divorce are often sad, withdrawn, and distracted—at the very time when children most need their love, support, and attention. Understandably, as a result of their parents' behavior, the children may feel that they no longer matter to them and that their parents no longer care about them. However, this is not the case—their parents are simply caught up in their own problems and struggling to deal with difficult emotions.

PAINFUL FEELINGS

Children going through a family breakup often feel let down, hurt, and deeply **betrayed** by the very people who are supposed to provide them with **security** and love: their parents. As a result, it is natural to feel anger, confusion, and sometimes even hatred toward one's mom and dad. However, it helps to remember that parents never make the decision to break up a family and end their relationship lightly. They have often taken a long time to come to their decision, and they have realized that they will be better parents to their children if they are happier apart from each other.

"I felt so confused—one minute I was sad, the next I was mad."

It is normal for children to feel let down by their parents when going through a family breakup.

Doing something physical can help children deal with feelings of anger.

Young people sometimes feel guilty because they may feel their behavior led to their parents' breakup. They may assume that their acting out at home, arguing and answering back, or fighting with their siblings has led to their parents breaking up. However, it is important for children to remember that the adults' relationship is not a child's responsibility.

GETTING THROUGH

For a while during the family breakup, children may feel very lonely and find it hard to continue with everyday life, such as schoolwork and extracurricular activities and hobbies. However, talking to others, such as trained counselors, other family members, and friends, can help put all of these troubling and upsetting feelings into **perspective**. The good news is that the difficult feelings, no matter how painful they are to experience, do pass in time. People can and do get through family breakups and feel happy again.

IT HAPPENED TO THEM

Selena Gomez was just five years old when her parents divorced. Growing up, Selma blamed her mom for the breakup. The actress and singer says that she now understands it was not her mom's fault, but instead, the young single mother did her best to raise her daughter. Selma says that she now defends young, single parents because she appreciates the sacrifices that her mother made for her.

GROWING UP HURTS

Life as a teenager is about growing up, becoming more independent, and discovering your identity as a young adult. It's an exciting time— but not always an easy one, because it may be packed with emotional and physical difficulty. An adolescent desperately needs their home to be a place of **stability** and security. However, when a parent leaves, a teenager's world becomes scary, uncertain, and confusing. It is rocked to the very core.

FEELING CONFUSED

A teenager can feel abandoned and **rejected** when a parent leaves. Feeling confused and unhappy, the teenager may then try and ignore these troublesome emotions and "switch off." They may become withdrawn, not want to speak, and seem distant to their parents. They may try to separate from the upset they are experiencing by using drugs or alcohol. Reliance on such substances may help a person forget their troubles in the short term. However, it **inevitably** leads to worse and more damaging problems in the long run, including serious physical and mental health problems.

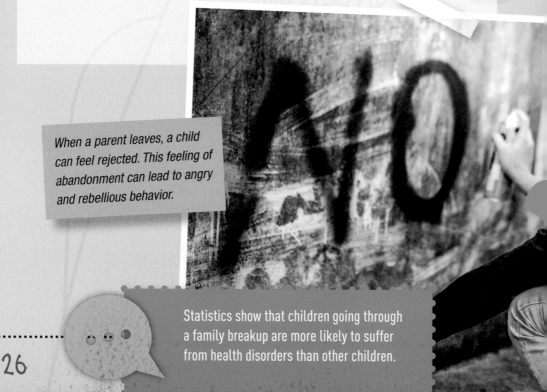

When a parent leaves, a child can feel rejected. This feeling of abandonment can lead to angry and rebellious behavior.

Statistics show that children going through a family breakup are more likely to suffer from health disorders than other children.

FEELING ANGRY

A young person may feel angry and begin to behave badly during a family breakup. Without the support of two parents, they may start to act in a more aggressive or rebellious way. They may act out at home and at school as a way to deal with the difficult emotions they face. Some teenagers do not show their upset in an aggressive manner but instead will blame themselves for their parents' problems. They may direct their anger toward themselves. This can lead to very self-destructive actions, such as **self-harming** or **eating disorders**. It is important to remember that, from anger and hatred to sadness and despair, the feelings surrounding family breakup are very painful but also very natural. They will pass in time, but talking about them can help people cope with a difficult situation.

Some children bottle up painful emotions, rather than showing them through outwardly destructive behavior.

IT HAPPENED TO THEM

Harry Styles' parents separated when he was seven. The singer says that his parents tried hard to make the split as easy as possible for him. Harry says that he stayed close to both his parents after the breakup and that he has always felt loved and supported by them.

NEEDING BOTH PARENTS

Keeping in touch with both parents is important for children. However, unfortunately, sometimes this may not be easy or even possible because of circumstances after a family breakup. For example, if one parent moves away, it may be difficult for them to maintain contact with children. However, after a separation or divorce, it is often possible for children to keep in touch and maintain their relationship with the absent parent, even if the adults want nothing more to do with each other.

WANTING TO STAY AWAY

Sometimes, a young person may choose not to keep in touch with a parent after they have moved away. They may feel too angry and hurt about the breakup, finding it easier to stop contact with the absent parent as a result. Even if a child feels this way, they may still have strong, loving feelings toward the absent parent and may miss them deeply. This confusion of feelings can be difficult to understand. However, in time, the young person may decide to renew communication, and the parent and child may develop a strong and loving relationship once more.

IT HAPPENS

Grandparents don't stop being grandparents just because their son's or daughter's relationship breaks down. They continue to love their grandchildren and want contact with them. However, it may not be easy for them to see their grandchildren regularly, particularly if their son or daughter does not have joint custody. Today, every US state has a law regarding grandparent **visitation** that can allow a judge to demand regular access to grandchildren.

RAW EMOTIONS

It is not just the relationship with the absent parent that presents challenges for families involved in breakups. For example, the parent with whom children live most of the time is usually responsible for the most difficult aspects of parenting, such as telling children to straighten rooms, do homework, and stick to curfews. It's easy to feel frustrated and angry with this parent because they present children with irritating rules and daily arguments. Unfortunately, the parent doing the daily caring for the children is usually the one who is the target of all **resentful** feelings and criticism, too!

Young people sometimes swing back and forth between feelings of love, sorrow, anger, and hatred for each parent. This perplexing mix of feelings does become less raw as time goes on, and children can gradually find new ways of communicating with and loving both parents.

Grandparents and other relatives can provide a safety net for children during troubling times.

COVID-19 has led to a surge in family breakup cases, with many people reporting the difficulties of being confined to their homes because of lockdowns and the domino effect this has had on their family relationships.

29

I'm So Scared

MONDAY JUNE 7

It's happening again. Mom is crying downstairs, and Ryan is yelling. I can hear him hitting her. I want to help Mom, but I'm so scared, too. I just want Ryan to stop.

WEDNESDAY JUNE 16

My teacher, Mrs. Montgomery, called Mom in to school today. Mom says she told her I've been acting weird at school, all sad and keeping away from the other kids. I had to go and see Mrs. Montgomery on my own at recess. She said she talked to Mom, and Mom told her that things are hard at home. Mrs. Montgomery gave me a hug and said she is always here for me, and I can talk to her whenever I want. I cried a little. That made me mad—it makes me look like a girl! Mrs. Montgomery told me that it is good to cry, and that real men cry. I told her Ryan says real men don't cry. She looked mad then.

SATURDAY JULY 3

Today, Ryan hit Mom again. Really bad. I screamed at Ryan and went for him. I hit him and yelled at him. Then Ryan shouted that he'd get me. Mom screamed at me to run outside. I ran to Ben's house and banged on his door. His mom opened the door—she looked shocked when she saw me. She said I looked terrified. Ben's mom grabbed me and pulled me inside. I told her what had happened, and she called the police. They came really fast, and they had Mom in the car. Mom said Ryan had run at the first sign of the police! Ben's mom was so nice—she said we could stay with her until it was safe to go home.

SUNDAY AUGUST 8

Mom and me moved back in today. No one has seen Ryan since the day he left, so we think it's safe to go home. We have changed the locks, too. Ben's mom and dad helped us move back in. Ben's mom

says she doesn't think we'll see Ryan again now. He'll be too scared of the police, and everyone knowing what he has done. I can't believe he is gone. Ben's mom says that this is a new beginning for us. She says that we can stop being scared and start living a normal life. She smiled at me and gave me a big hug when she said that.

TUESDAY SEPTEMBER 14
Mrs. Montgomery talked to us all about family breakups at school today. She said that a lot of kids go through family breakups, and that it helps to talk about it. She explained that families break up for all kinds of reasons. She said breakups can be sad, then she looked at me and said, but sometimes they can make things better, too. She's right. I'm so glad Ryan's gone.

I hate listening to Ryan shouting at Mom. I want to make him stop, but I'm really scared of him, too.

CHAPTER FOUR

CHANGING LIVES

The change in one family is often the beginning of another, new family, and though this may be exciting, it can also feel daunting and overwhelming for everyone involved—parents and children alike. However, new families present particular challenges for children.

NEW RELATIONSHIP

It's not easy to accept your mom or dad meeting and dating a new partner. Children often feel strongly that their parent should stay single, and they may still hope for their parents' **reconciliation** and for their broken family to **reunite**. A new partner puts an end to that hope. Things can also be further complicated if a new partner was the cause of the parents' separation. The children might feel resentful toward the new adult in their lives because they blame them for their family breakup and the pain that it has caused them.

SOMEONE NEW

When a new partner comes on the scene, it's easy for a child to compare them to the absent parent—often unfavorably! However, these feelings can usually be overcome if the new partner makes a concerted effort to try and build their own, unique relationship with any children, rather than attempting to replace a much-loved parent. Inevitably, that will only lead to further resentment and hostility.

IT HAPPENS

Stepfamilies have gotten particularly bad press in literature. Just think of Cinderella's cruel stepmother and taunting stepsisters, or Snow White's jealous stepmother. It's not easy for any woman or man to take on the role of stepparent. They may not have had experience with children and may be very worried about forming relationships with the children of a new partner. Accepting a stepparent doesn't mean that a child is being disloyal to the natural parent—it just means they are learning to manage new relationships.

Families work best if everyone tries hard to build strong relationships.

Blended or stepfamilies often come with stepbrothers or stepsisters. This can add to the problems of the new family because it means getting along with yet more people. Not only have the children had to form a relationship with their parent's new partner, now they must form one with their children! Children may find themselves sharing their home and parent with other children whom they hardly know, and such relationships take time to adjust to. Talking calmly and honestly about feelings can help prevent a buildup of resentment or bad feeling in these extremely challenging situations.

It's not easy to accept your mom or dad meeting ... a new partner.

MANAGING TO LIVE

Running a household on just one income is much harder than it is when two adults are contributing to the budget. There is often less money to live on, and the family may need to move somewhere where living costs are less expensive.

Parents who split up often continue to argue after their split—now about money and how much each parent should put in toward the costs of raising children and running a home. Another factor that also influences the situation is that one or both parents may be in new relationships and now having to help support their stepchildren. If money is already tight in these new family situations, having to contribute toward the upkeep of their ex-partner's home creates additional strain and tension, and arguments can get out of control as a result.

When parents are having trouble with their own emotions, it can be hard to give children the emotional support they need.

IT HAPPENS

Parents who don't live with their children for the majority of the time may try and make up for the lost time by showering their children with lots of gifts. Unfortunately, this can cause resentment with the other parent, and it does not improve the lives of the children, either. Although children love gifts, they usually prefer to have quality time with their parent, hanging out and talking.

LIFE BECOMES TOUGH

Single parents often have to work extremely long hours to earn enough money to make the payments on their **mortgage** or to cover the costs of the rent, bills, and food and clothing for their children. This intense and often exhausting work schedule often means they have less time to spend with their children, and when they are with their children, the parents may be too tired to offer them the quality attention that they would like. This lack of time can be extremely difficult for the parent, who misses their children while they are at work and may feel guilty that they are not spending more time with them.

Adjusting to life after a breakup is also difficult for the children, who now more than ever need attention and love from their parent. The children may feel unhappy because things seem to be getting harder rather than easier now that their parents have separated. They are aware that their parent is not as available to them as they were before, and that work is necessarily taking priority. Under these extremely stressful and challenging circumstances, it is more important than ever that parents and children continue to talk, so that everyone is aware of the challenges faced and can try and see things from a different point of view.

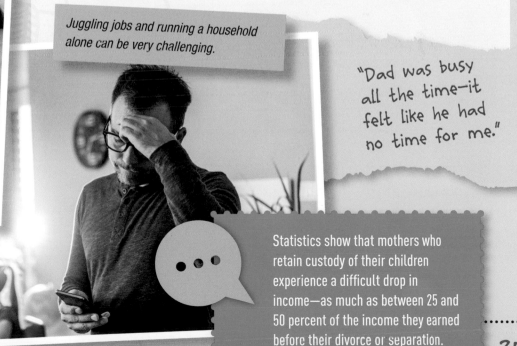

Juggling jobs and running a household alone can be very challenging.

"Dad was busy all the time—it felt like he had no time for me."

Statistics show that mothers who retain custody of their children experience a difficult drop in income—as much as between 25 and 50 percent of the income they earned before their divorce or separation.

TAKING CONTROL

Young people may not be able to step in and fix their parents' relationship, but they can help take control of the way they handle a family breakup and take care of their physical and mental well-being. Focusing on positive activities, such as meeting friends or playing sports, can help them forget about the negativity in their lives and put thinking about their problems on hold for awhile.

It's important to be open and honest about feelings—however, it is understandable if young people don't want to talk to their parents about how they feel when a family breakup is underway. They may feel that talking to one parent would be disloyal to the other, for example, or they may feel guilty about their feelings of resentment toward their parents. Sometimes, they may simply feel too angry to talk to them. Talking to friends or trusted adults rather than parents can help bring a sense of perspective to an upsetting situation and help young people air their concerns and emotions. There are usually counselors at school who can offer support and advice, too.

Counseling can help children process emotions about their family's breakup.

Overall, 2.2 percent of all parents split up, and married and cohabiting couples split up, at an annual rate of 1.3 percent and 5.3 percent respectively.

HOW NOT TO HELP!

Aunts, uncles, other relatives, and family friends often want to help and offer support to children going through family breakups. However, it is important that they give the right kind of support and help. It is not helpful if they say unkind and hurtful things about one of the parents involved, for example—and it's perfectly fine for children to ask their relatives not to criticize their parents.

It can be difficult for young people to witness families around them that are still intact when theirs has broken up. For example, some young people might feel jealous of friends whose parents are still together, and they may feel angry that their parents aren't able to get along as well as other people's parents who have separated. It is important to remember that every family is different, and comparing them won't help build new and lasting relationships in the changed family.

IT HAPPENS

People don't forget or "get over" it when parents separate, but they can come to terms with the breakup and find ways to create positive, new family relationships. Relationships change all the time, and while a family breakup forces people to build different kinds of relationships with parents, it can also be an opportunity to make stronger, better relationships. Adjusting to change isn't easy, and it takes time. However, the good news is that in some breakup cases, young people find that their parents are much happier apart. This optimism makes everyone's relationships easier and more positive in the long run.

This Is All His Fault

FRIDAY APRIL 2

It's Dad's turn to have us this weekend. I don't want to go. Mom says I have to, and that we must stick to what the court agreed—that Dad would have us over every other weekend. I just want to stay here. Dad's house is on the other side of town. All my friends are here. When Dad picked me up after school, I just threw my bag in the car and didn't look at him. I hate him. This is all his fault. He was the one who wanted to split up, not Mom.

I just want things to be how they used to be—before Dad ruined our lives.

SATURDAY APRIL 3

Dad told me to come out of my room and mix with the rest of the family. Yeah, right! They aren't my family. Dad's girlfriend, Rachel, has two bratty kids that are way younger than me. Chloe is four, and Isaac is eight. I hate Rachel, too. It's her fault that Mom and Dad split. If it wasn't for her, Dad would still be at home.

SUNDAY APRIL 4

We had to go to the park today, so dorky Isaac and Chloe could play. Rachel was laughing and acting like we are one big happy family. Dad kept looking at her, all mushy. I sat on the swings and just listened to my music. Can't wait to go home. When we got back to the house, I just went back to my room and locked the door. Felt better after a couple of beers.
If Dad catches me drinking, he'll go nuts. I don't care.

MONDAY MAY 3

School was good today—I hung out with some new guys at recess. They said they know where I can get as much beer as I want—drugs, too, if I want them. Dad called Mom later and told her Rachel had found a beer can in my room. Mom put Dad on the phone, and he gave me a stupid lecture about drinking and drugs, and how they mess up your life. I told him he can't tell me what to do—and that he has messed up my life already, totally.

SATURDAY JUNE 12

Dad came over to our house tonight to talk to Mom. He says he is worried about me. He told Mom that I'm drinking a lot, and that I keep hanging out with older guys near his house. Mom and Dad told me they want us all to go to **family therapy**. I yelled at them that we aren't a family anymore—not since Dad decided to bust us up! They can make me do therapy … but it won't change anything.

CHAPTER FIVE

CHANGING FAMILIES

After the **social revolution** of the 1960s, some couples began to live together without marrying. However, up until the mid-1990s, it was still unusual for a couple to live together unless they were married—and it was very unusual for a child's parents to be unmarried. Today, things have changed almost beyond **recognition**.

These days, families may have one parent, stepparents, two moms, two dads … the family setup may be much more flexible, but it is no less important than it was before. With so much change, it has become essential that people recognize that families have new structures, and that they show respect and consideration for each type of family. Thankfully, today, there is much more acceptance of different family setups than there used to be in the past. People have become aware that what is important is that family members show each other kindness and support, whatever the family structure.

As long as children feel happy and loved, they can safely explore the world and develop into confident young people.

There are 11.6 million stepchildren in the United States. It is estimated that around 113 million Americans have a step relationship: 13 percent are stepparents, 15 percent are stepdads, and 12 percent are stepmoms.

IT HAPPENS

In the 1970s, there was a rise in the number of divorces. There were several possible reasons for this rise. First, changes in the law made it easier to get a divorce, and women began to earn more. Second, with more financial independence, women could realistically consider supporting their family alone. Although the United States remains in the top five countries with the highest divorce rates (3.6 for every 1,000 people), today the divorce rate is falling. This drop could be because fewer people are marrying and many cohabit instead—or it could be because many couples decide to settle down together when they are older, and these relationships tend to last longer. There are many ways to interpret the figures on family breakup, but what matters most is that in each family, children are loved, cared for, and safe.

Some people argue that families are more likely to break up today because women can work and earn their own money.

A LOT OF BAD PRESS

Newspaper headlines sometimes scream that single-parent families are responsible for many social problems, from **social unrest** and street crime to alcohol and drug addiction, teenage pregnancies, and high school dropouts. There is often a lot of sensational and negative press around "broken" homes, which are regularly blamed for the behavior of unruly children. These negative **stereotypes** are not helpful—and they are not accurate in many cases. Thankfully, today, many people are beginning to challenge such stereotypes, and slowly, attitudes to families are changing.

A REALLY TOUGH JOB

Being a parent can be really tough, but it is even harder when there is only one parent to support and care for the children. It is also extremely difficult to bring up children in a family in which both parents live together, but constantly fight and argue. Growing up in either of these family situations is not easy, and children within broken homes, or homes that are experiencing conflict and **turbulence**, can find life extremely challenging.

Dealing with change can be difficult, but children who grow up feeling safe, secure, and confident can go on to lead very successful lives.

Negative stereotypes are not helpful ...

It is important to remember that a successful family structure can take any form.

However, just because a child has experienced family breakup, it doesn't automatically mean that he or she will suffer at school or later in life. Their life chances are not solely based on their family environment and their upbringing. Nor does it mean that the child will inevitably turn to drugs or alcohol—any of these things can happen to anyone, regardless of their family setup and background. More important than any family arrangement and structure is the love and support a child receives at home, and from the parent or parents with whom they have contact. That is the key to their happiness, well-being, and future success.

IT HAPPENED TO THEM

Perhaps one of the most famous examples of someone who has come through a family breakup and gone on to become an enormous success is Barack Obama. Barack's parents separated when he was two years old. Then, at the age of 10, he went to live with his grandmother, who brought him up for the remainder of his childhood. Obama went on to twice become president of the United States! His example proves that a child who has experienced family breakup will not necessarily turn out to be troubled and a low achiever—they may in fact go on to take on roles of key importance in the world.

Working It Out

AMY'S STORY
SUNDAY FEBRUARY 5

Dad came over to see us this weekend. He says that he's feeling a lot better. Dad told me that he was really depressed after losing his job, and that he couldn't deal with how he felt. I hugged him and said I knew he was sad, and pretending that everything was OK just made it all worse for me. Dad says that he'll always tell me the truth from now on.

Mom and Dad have been talking, too. Mom says a counselor is helping them figure out their problems. I asked if Dad might move home. Mom said we need to take it one step at a time, but she was smiling when she said it. Dad says that whatever happens, we will all be OK. And I believe him.

ZOE'S STORY
MONDAY MARCH 14

Mom has been back home now for a couple of months. At first, I was so mad that I didn't talk to her. Dad told Mom that I just needed time—that it had been so hard for me when she left.

Aunt Julie planned for me to see a counselor, Meghan. She was so nice, she just let me talk about how I felt, how I hated Mom. Then Mom told me that her doctor thinks she has had **postnatal depression,** that sometimes when women have babies, it can make them really sad. That made me see things differently. Slowly, I've stopped being so mad at Mom. Today, we went to see Meghan together. Mom cried when I told her how her leaving had made me feel. And she hugged me when I said I don't hate her anymore.

Amy: I'm glad I kept my journal. Reading it makes me realize how bad I felt when Dad left. I don't want to feel like that ever again.

ZAK'S STORY
SATURDAY DECEMBER 25

Best Christmas ever! I got a new Playstation! Mom said I could play all day! I could never have done that when Ryan was here. We went over to Ben's house for lunch. Ben's mom and dad are so cool. They let me sleep over some nights since Ryan left, so Mom could go out. I was worried at first. I didn't want Mom to get another loser boyfriend like Ryan. But Mom says she only wants one man in her life—me!

I still get scared that Ryan will come back. Every night, I check that the doors are locked, and if a car pulls up, it spooks me. Mom says she feels the same, but in time, we'll both stop feeling scared.

JOE'S STORY
SATURDAY OCTOBER 16

I went to Dad and Rachel's today. It was still pretty lame, and Chloe and Isaac are still annoying, but at least Dad isn't making me go to the park with them anymore.

Our family therapist, Jake, says Dad needs to understand how I feel and respect it. I thought therapy would be useless—wrong! Jake is great —he says I can say what I want, and that I won't be in trouble. I said that I think everything is Dad's fault, and Jake says that's OK. I've agreed with Jake to talk rather than drink so much now. I still think the split is Dad's fault, but I don't hate him as much anymore.

GLOSSARY

abusers people who carry out physically or emotionally harmful behavior

abusive physically or emotionally harmful behavior

access able to have contact

bereavement losing someone through death

betrayed let down

blended families families that are made up of a couple and the children they have had from previous relationships

custody the legal right to care for a child or children

depression a mental illness that causes severe sadness

domestic abuse physical or emotional abuse that takes place within a relationship

eating disorders unhealthy relationships with food, such as anorexia nervosa

family therapy talking as a family group about problems with a trained professional

foster families families in which children are cared for by people who are not their parents for a period of time

inevitably impossible to change

judgments conclusions made in court by a judge

mediation intervention, or stepping in, to try to resolve a situation

mortgage money borrowed to buy a property, which must be paid back to the lender monthly

perspective a point of view

postnatal depression an intense feeling of sadness experienced by some women after childbirth

psychological related to the mind

recognition recognizing and identifying something or someone

reconciliation coming together again

rejected turned away and given up

relocation moving to a new area

resentful feeling unfairly treated

resilient able to cope with difficulties

resolution finding a solution and bringing a problem to an end

resolve to end a problem

reunite to bring together again

security safe from harm

self-harming hurting oneself, often by cutting the skin

social revolution a movement in society to bring about big changes

social unrest feelings of unhappiness and the demonstration about it in a community

stability stable, not unsettled

stereotypes widely held but inaccurate beliefs about people

turbulence unsettled situations

unconditional without conditions

visitation allowed by law to visit a child or children

withdrawn not wanting to communicate with other people

FIND OUT MORE

BOOKS

Callahan, Timothy, and Claudia Isler. *A Teen's Guide to Custody* (Divorce and Your Family). Rosen Publishing, 2016.

Jones, Viola. *Divorce and Your Family* (Divorce and Your Feelings). Rosen Publishing, 2017.

Morrow, Paula. *My Parents Are Divorcing. Now What?* (Teen Life 411). Rosen Publishing, 2015.

WEBSITES

For help with managing difficult emotions related to divorce in your family, visit:
iamachildofdivorce.com

Learn more about divorce and family breakups at:
kidshealth.org/en/kids/divorce.html

Discover how to deal with difficult emotions at:
kidshelpline.com.au/teens/issues/coping-emotions

ORGANIZATIONS

Teen Line
Cedars-Sinai
P.O. Box 48750
Los Angeles, CA 90048
(310) 855-HOPE (4673) or
(800) TLC-TEEN (852-8336)
Website: teenlineonline.org
If you are struggling with a family breakup, or know someone who is, help is out there. Connect and get support at this great help site for teenagers.

PUBLISHER'S NOTE TO EDUCATORS AND PARENTS:

All the websites featured above have been carefully reviewed to ensure that they are suitable for students. However, many websites change often, and we cannot guarantee that a site's future contents will continue to meet our high standards of educational value. Please be advised that students should be closely monitored whenever they access the Internet.

INDEX

ABOUT THE AUTHORS

Sarah Eason has authored many nonfiction books for children and has a special interest in young people's health and social issues. Sarah Levete has written hundreds of information books for children on a wide variety of subjects, including health and well-being.